I USE MATH

I USE MATH IN THE WORKSHOP

by Joanne Mattern
Reading consultant: Susan Nations, M.Ed., author/literacy coach/consultant

WR WEEKLY READER
EARLY LEARNING LIBRARY

Please visit our web site at: www.earlyliteracy.cc
For a free color catalog describing Weekly Reader® Early Learning Library's list
of high-quality books, call 1-877-445-5824 (USA) or 1-800-387-3178 (Canada).
Weekly Reader® Early Learning Library's fax: (414) 336-0164.

Library of Congress Cataloging-in-Publication Data available upon request from publisher.
Fax (414) 336-0157 for the attention of the Publishing Records Department.

ISBN 0-8368-4858-6 (lib. bdg.)
ISBN 0-8368-4865-9 (softcover)

This edition first published in 2006 by
Weekly Reader® Early Learning Library
A Member of the WRC Media Family of Companies
330 West Olive Street, Suite 100
Milwaukee, WI 53212 USA

Managing editor: Valerie J. Weber
Art direction: Tammy West
Cover design and page layout: Dave Kowalski
Photo research: Diane Laska-Swanke
Photographer: Gregg Andersen

Printed in the United States of America

1 2 3 4 5 6 7 8 9 09 08 07 06 05

Note to Educators and Parents

Reading is such an exciting adventure for young children! They are beginning to integrate their oral language skills with written language. To encourage children along the path to early literacy, books must be colorful, engaging, and interesting; they should invite the young reader to explore both the print and the pictures.

I Use Math is a new series designed to help children read about using math in their everyday lives. In each book, young readers will explore a different activity and solve math problems along the way.

Each book is specially designed to support the young reader in the reading process. The familiar topics are appealing to young children and invite them to read — and reread — again and again. The full-color photographs and enhanced text further support the student during the reading process.

In addition to serving as wonderful picture books in schools, libraries, homes, and other places where children learn to love reading, these books are specifically intended to be read within an instructional guided reading group. This small group setting allows beginning readers to work with a fluent adult model as they make meaning from the text. After children develop fluency with the text and content, the book can be read independently. Children and adults alike will find these books supportive, engaging, and fun!

— Susan Nations, M.Ed., author, literacy coach,
and consultant in literacy development

I like to build! Today, Dad and I are making a bird house. We need five pieces of wood to build the house. We need two pieces of wood to build the roof.

How many pieces of wood are on the table?

I measure the
wood to make sure
it is the right size.

How long is the wood?

7

Dad cuts the wood.
He must be careful.
That saw is sharp.

What shape is the wood Dad is sawing?

9

I am gluing the pieces
of the house together.
I have glued three sides
to the base so far.

How many pieces still need to be glued on?

Dad helps me put the roof together. Our hands must be steady while the glue dries.

Can you see what shape the two sides of the roof will form?

We also need a lot of nails to put our bird house together. I count each nail to make sure we have enough.

Each pack has ten nails.
How many packs hold thirty nails?

14

I like to hammer!
The noise is pretty loud!

I hit one nail five times.
How many times will I hit four nails?

The birds need a place to stand. Dad cuts a piece of wood. He glues it to the house.

Dad cut an eight-inch piece of wood in half. How long was each piece?

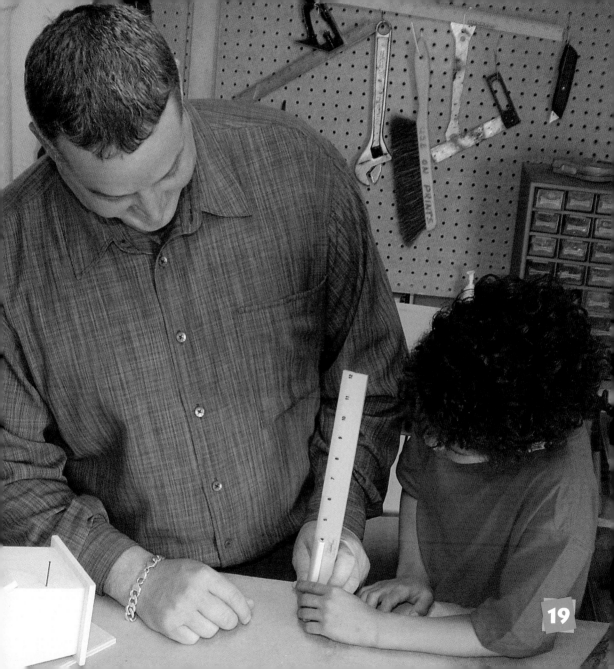

Our bird house is done!

We started making the bird house at 2:00. Now it is 3:00. How long did it take to make the bird house?

Glossary

build — to make something by putting parts together

hammer — a tool used for hitting nails

measure — to find out the size of something

nails — small, pointed pieces of metal

pieces — parts of something larger

Answers

Page 4 – 7

Page 6 – 6 inches

Page 8 – rectangle

Page 10 – 3

Page 12 – a triangle

Page 14 – 3

Page 16 – 20

Page 18 – 4 inches

Page 20 – 1 hour

For More Information

Books

Carpenters. Community Helpers (series).
  Debbie L. Yanuck (Bridgestone Books)
Measurement and Units. Science Factory (series).
  Jon Richards (Copper Beech)
Measuring. I Can Do Math (series).
  Marcia S. Gresko (Gareth Stevens Publishing)
Measuring: The Perfect Playhouse. Math Monsters
  (series). John Burstein (Weekly Reader® Early
  Learning Library)

Websites

Bluebird Nesting Box
www.pawtographs.com/html/bird_house_plans.html
Follow these plans with an adult to build
a bird house.

Index

About the Author

Joanne Mattern is the author of more than 130 books for children. Her favorite subjects are animals, history, sports, and biography. Joanne lives in New York State with her husband, three young daughters, and three crazy cats.